Fun with Electronics

by Conn McQuinn

Illustrations by Kaz Aizawa

Andrews and McMeel

A Universal Press Syndicate Company

Kansas City

HEY! I'M A CIRCUIT!

To Betsy, Caitlin, and Alec Curran.
Thanks for keeping my batteries charged.

The *Fun with Electronics* packaged set is produced by becker&mayer!, Ltd.

Fun with Electronics copyright © 1994 by becker&mayer!, Ltd. Project illustrations copyright © 1994 by Kaz Aizawa. All rights reserved. Printed in USA. No part of this book may be used or reproduced in any manner whatsoever without written permission except in the case of reprints in the context of reviews. For information, write Andrews and McMeel, a Universal Press Syndicate Company, 4520 Main Street, Kansas City, Missouri 64111.

From the *Fun with Electronics* packaged set, which includes electronic parts, electronic workbench, wires, and this book.

Assembly illustrations: Sylvia Shapiro
Electronic circuit design: Hunter Fulghum
Package and book design: Jane Kobayashi

First printing, May 1994

Fourth printing, June 1997

Fun with Electronics

ISBN: 0-8362-4231-9

Other children's kits by becker&mayer!:
The Amazing Sandcastle Builder's Kit
The American Appaloosa
The Ant Book & See-Through Model
Build Your Own Dinosaurs
The English Thoroughbred
Fun with Ballet
Sleeping Beauty

Contents

What's Electricity?	**5**
Putting Together the Workbench	**7**
Testing Your Workbench	**18**
Troubleshooting	**20**
Note to Parents	**21**
#1 Engine Sounds	**22**
#2 Siren with Light	**24**
#3 Light Fader	**26**
#4 Traffic Light	**28**
#5 Burglar Alarm	**30**
#6 Musical Organ	**32**
#7 Touch-Activated Switch	**34**
#8 Sound-Activated Switch	**36**
#9 Light-Activated Switch	**38**
#10 Light Organ	**40**
#11 Electronic Timer	**42**
#12 Electronic Candle	**44**
#13 Conductance Checker	**46**
#14 Strength Detector	**48**
#15 Electronic Rooster	**50**
#16 Electronic Tag	**52**
#17 Morse Code Generator	**54**
#18 Intercom	**56**
#19 Metronome	**58**
#20 Crystal Radio	**60**
#21 Transistor Radio	**62**
#22 Electronic Thermometer	**64**
#23 Flip-Flop Circuit	**66**
#24 Persistence-of-Vision Tester	**68**
#25 Metal Detector	**70**

Welcome to
Fun with Electronics

This book (and all that stuff in the plastic box) will let you put together and experiment with a number of different electrical projects. You will build burglar alarms, radios, timers, and all sorts of really fun things that will amaze and astound your friends and family. Okay, so maybe they won't be amazed and astounded, but they *will* be impressed.

Before you can do these projects, however, you need to prepare your Electronic Workbench. You will do this by installing all of the little electronic parts in the plastic container onto the cardboard box with the holes punched in it. Once all of the **components** (that means "electronic parts") are installed, then you will make your projects by hooking the components together with pieces of wire. Each project is a different **circuit**, a term that means "a bunch of electronic components that does something when you send electricity through it." This one basic setup will let you build 25 different circuits.

MY FINEST CREATION!

What's Electricity?

ELECTRICITY

Of course, none of these projects will do a thing without **electricity**. So just what is electricity?

Everything you see around you — and a lot of stuff you can't see, like air — is made up of atoms. Atoms have **electrons**. Under the right conditions and with the right materials, these electrons can be made to jump from one atom to another. When you have a bunch of electrons moving in the same direction, it's called electricity or an **electrical current**.

Why would the electrons be moving? Sometimes there are too many electrons in one place, so they try to move somewhere else. You've probably had it happen to you. When you walk along a wool carpet on a dry day, your feet scrape electrons off of the atoms in the carpet, and they all go into your body. All those extra electrons want to go someplace where it isn't so crowded, so when you reach for a doorknob (or another person), they jump. That big crowd of electrons moving at once makes a spark, and a **snap**, and you've just demonstrated electrical current! (Usually followed by jumping up and down, shaking your finger, and yelling "Ooo, I just *hate that*!")

As the word **current** might tell you, people compare electricity to water. It "flows" through certain kinds of materials, called **conductors**. But instead of using plumbing, you build circuits.

Most of the components in your Electronic Workbench are things that change the flow of electricity. Some slow it down, some work like one-way valves, some work like faucet controls, and so on. The wires act like pipes to connect them all together.

For all of your circuits (except one!) the electricity will come from a battery acting as an electricity pump. It has a lot of extra electrons in one side, and not enough on the other side.

When you connect the battery **terminals** (the metal parts on top), the electrons flow from one terminal to the other. In your projects, the electricity will travel from the *negative* terminal (too many electrons) to the *positive* terminal (not enough electrons).

Warning #1: Do not use any other source of electricity with your projects. The current from wall sockets or appliances is very, very strong and can cause you great injury. There is no risk from the current in your battery, but anything more powerful will at the very least damage the circuits in your Electronic Workbench. Or it could damage *your* circuits. **Treat electricity *with extreme care.***

Putting Together the Workbench

Warning #2: Do not just connect the two terminals of the battery directly together with a piece of wire or other metal. The battery and wire will heat up enough to burn you!

PUTTING TOGETHER THE BASIC ELECTRONIC WORKBENCH

Part of this kit is a cardboard box with lots of holes punched in it. This box will form the base to the many cool circuits that you will build. The first step in transforming the box into your Electronic Workbench is installing the springs that you will find in the plastic case.

The springs are just the right size to fit into the large holes punched in the top of the cardboard box. Some of the holes

might not be all the way punched through, so take a pen or pencil and push the extra cardboard through the hole. Then

push a spring about halfway into each of the 52 bigger holes (they have a number next to them). There should be enough springs to fill all 52 holes. After you have filled all the holes with springs, open the bottom of the box so you can put the rest of the parts together.

You are now ready to begin installing your components, but first these **Words of Warning: Many of these parts will not**

The Capacitors

work if they are not put in the right way, and *some will get permanently zapped if they are put in wrong.* Pay close attention to the directions or you'll be trotting down to your local electronic-supply store for replacement parts!

PART ONE: THE CAPACITORS

The first parts that you are going to install are called **capacitors**. These guys act as little electricity storage tanks. They come in thousands of sizes and kinds, and are used mainly to provide a place in a circuit where the power of the electricity can build up to a higher level. Capacitors are also very helpful in smoothing out any variations in the power of the electricity, sort of like electrical shock absorbers. All of the capacitors have numbers on

the side that indicate how much electricity the capacitor will hold. They're measured in units called "Farads," which are named after a man named Faraday. (I personally think they should call them "Faradays," but they decided this about two hundred years ago, and I didn't get a vote.)

You have five different capacitors for your workbench. Three of them look like little brown disks (almost like tiny M&M's) with two leads sticking out. These are called **ceramic capacitors**. If you look closely, you will see that there is printing on the side. Find the smallest one — it should say "102" on it. This is going to be the first component that you install. Follow these steps!

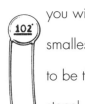

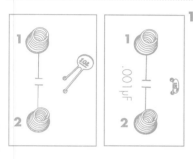

1. Put the leads from the bottom of the capacitor through the small holes next to springs 1 and 2. It doesn't make any difference which lead goes in which hole.

2. Turn the box over and bend spring 1 until you can insert the closest lead into one of the gaps. Once you have the wire lead in spring 1, let go of the spring.

3. Put the other lead into spring 2.

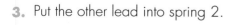

Congratulations! You have just installed your first part! (Only 21 more to go!)

Now that you have the basic idea, the rest of the parts should go fairly quickly, *but pay close attention to the directions!* (Do I sound like your mother or what?)

4. Take the capacitor numbered "103" or ".01" and install it into the holes and springs numbered 3 and 4.

5. Put the capacitor numbered "503" or ".05" into holes and springs 5 and 6.

The other two capacitors look like small, dark blue cans with two leads on the bottom. These are **elec-trolytic capacitors**. They store more electricity than

The Resistors

ceramic capacitors. Another important difference is that these capacitors **don't work if you put them in backwards**. Find the capacitor that says "47uF" on the side. Look carefully, and you should be able to find one side that has a minus (-) sign on it. Put the lead under the minus sign through the small hole next to spring 8 and the other lead through the small hole next to spring 7. Attach them to the springs underneath. Now double-check and make sure that the minus side of the capacitor is next to spring 8. (Nag, nag, nag.)

Now take the last capacitor (which should say "470uF" on the side) and put it into holes 9 and 10, with the lead from the minus side attaching to spring 10.

PART TWO: THE RESISTORS

Resistors are components that reduce the flow of electricity.

Even in materials that conduct electricity, there is always some *resistance* to the electricity. Resistance is like friction; it makes it hard to move the electricity through. Most of the time resistance is a problem, because it means that electricity is wasted.

But resistors are made to have a very specific level of resistance. They can be used to control how much electricity is traveling in a circuit, which is very important. Some of the compo-

green
brown
brown
gold or
silver

nents you have in your Electronic Workbench need only small amounts of electricity. The battery produces more than they need and without resistors they would burn out. The electricity straight from the battery would make some circuits run too fast to be usable, but the resistors slow down the flow to a useful level.

If you look carefully, you'll see that each resistor has colored stripes. The stripes indicate how strong the resistor is, and each color indicates a different number (except for a gold or silver one on the end). The stripes are pretty small, so you should try to work with a good light and look closely so you can tell the difference between a brown stripe and a purple stripe. You should have six resistors, and they should be installed as follows:

1. Find the resistor with green, brown, and brown stripes. (The last brown stripe should be closest to the gold or silver stripe). Install it in springs 11 and 12. It doesn't matter which way you put it in.

2. Install the resistor with brown, black, and red stripes in springs 13 and 14.

3. Install the resistor with green, brown, and red stripes in springs 15 and 16.

Transistors

4. Install the resistor with brown, black, and orange stripes in springs 17 and 18.

5. Install the resistor with brown, black, and yellow stripes in springs 19 and 20.

6. Install the resistor with yellow, purple, and yellow stripes in springs 21 and 22.

PART THREE: TRANSISTORS

There should be two small black components with three leads sticking out of the bottom. These are **tran-sistors.** There are only two in your Electronic Workbench, but they are very important. **They are also very easy to break, so be very careful!**

A small turn of the handle here...

...releases a large amount of water here.

Transistors work like small electricity faucets. The top leg is where electricity comes in, and the bottom leg is where electricity goes out. The middle leg turns the flow on and off. If just a little bit of electricity comes into the middle leg, it will open the transistor and let a lot of electricity flow from the top leg to the bottom leg. If the middle leg doesn't get any electricity, then no electricity goes through.

A small amount of electricity here...

...results in a large amount of electricity here.

Transistors play a huge part in most modern electronics. Here's how to install yours:

Other Stuff

1. The leads from the first transistor go into springs 23, 24, and 25. Hold the transistor so the curved side faces spring 23. Put the center lead into the hole next to spring 23, the lead closest to the top of the Electronic Workbench in the hole next to spring 24, and the lead closest to the bottom in the hole next to spring 25. (Better double-check that drawing.) Connect the leads to the springs.

2. Install the leads from the second transistor in springs 26, 27, and 28. Face the curved side toward spring 26, and put the center lead into hole 26. Put the top lead into hole 27, and the bottom lead into hole 28. Connect to the springs.

PART FOUR: ALL THAT OTHER STUFF

First in this group is the **diode,** a little glass tube with leads coming out of both ends. A diode is a "one-way" component like a valve — it lets electricity go through in one direction, but not the other. Attach this to springs 44 and 45, with the black stripe pointing at spring 45.

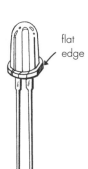

The bright red and green "lights" are called **light-emitting diodes,** or LEDs for short. Just like the plain vanilla diode you just installed, these allow electricity to go in only one direction. However, they also light up, which of course makes them way cooler.

flat edge

More Stuff

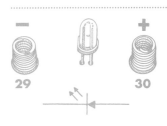

− 29   **+** 30

If you look at the LEDs carefully, you will notice that one side of the little edge around the bottom is flat. Put the red LED into springs 29 and 30, with the flat edge next to spring 29. Put the green LED into springs 31 and 32, with the flat side toward 31. Double-check the LEDs and the diode—if they're in backwards, they'll plug everything up!

The **photocell** is an orange disk with tiny stripes. This is actually a special kind of resistor that varies how much it resists depending on how much light is shining on it. The darker it gets in the room where you're working, the less electricity it lets through. All you need to do to install this is attach it to springs 46 and 47. It doesn't matter how you put it in. (Well, don't use a hammer or anything, I just meant it doesn't matter which lead goes on which spring.)

The funny-looking thing with five leads coming out of it is called a **transformer** (see drawing). (No, it doesn't turn into a robot. Be kinda cool if it did, though.) A transformer is a device that changes the voltage of the electricity passing through it. Put it in the holes indicated in the drawing (the leads will match up exactly with the small holes)

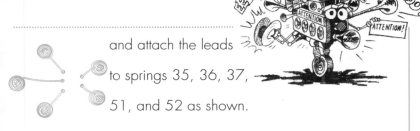

and attach the leads to springs 35, 36, 37, 51, and 52 as shown.

The big round metal disk is the *piezo transducer*. (That's pronounced pea - AY - zoh, just in case you wanted to know.) It makes noise when electricity goes through it. Place the two leads on the piezo transducer through the two holes next to springs 38 and 39 as shown, then attach the leads to springs 38 and 39, making sure the leads don't touch.

38

39

metal screw hole

The square, clear box is the *variable capacitor*. As the name implies, it is a capacitor that can be changed, which can be a very handy thing. On top of the box is a short metal tube with screw threads on the inside. From underneath the workbench, push the metal tube up through the hole to the right of springs 42 and 43 and hold it in place. Then place the round plastic knob on top of the tube, so that it notches into place. Use the special screw to attach the knob firmly to the metal tube. When you have the knob attached, carefully connect the wires on the bottom of the variable capacitor onto springs 42 and 43.

42

43

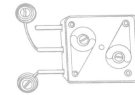

Even More Stuff

The black metal rod and coil of copper wire are the two parts of the **antenna**. The antenna picks up faint radio signals that you will actually be able to hear. To assemble the antenna, slide the coil of wire over the metal rod as shown. You may have to bend the coil into the shape of the metal rod. To put it in the Electronic Workbench,

48 49 50

look carefully at the workbench next to springs number 48, 49, and 50, and you will see two tabs that can be folded up. These tabs hold the antenna in place (please look at the drawing, because it's a lot easier to draw than explain). Once you have the antenna in place, put the three wires through the hole between springs 48 and 49. Then from the

red   no color   green

bottom, attach the red wire in spring 48, the uncolored wire in spring 49, and the green wire to spring 50. Only the very ends of the wire are bare metal, so make sure the metal ends are touching the springs.

The **earphone** looks like—wait a minute, you know what an earphone looks like! Anyway, this earphone actually has a small speaker inside it and can translate electricity into sound. To attach the earphone to the workbench, put the wire through the small hole

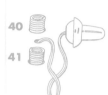

between springs 40 and 41 and attach the bare metal ends of the wire to those two springs, in no particular order.

And last, but certainly not least, is the **battery holder.** Feed the red and black leads through the small hole next to springs 33 and 34. The red wire goes to spring 33, and the black wire to spring 34. (Definitely double-check this, because if you did this backwards, *nothing's gonna work.*) Place a 9-volt battery into the punched-out rectangle. When you build a circuit, you will connect the battery clips to the battery.

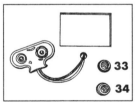

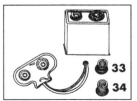

Whew! Congratulations! Your Electronic Workbench is done!

There will be a bunch of hookup wires left over, which you should keep in the plastic box. You will use them for building your projects, and they're pretty neat projects, too, if I do say so myself. However, there is one more step that we must take, and that is . . .

Testing Your Workbench

TESTING YOUR ELECTRONIC WORKBENCH

Before you get too far, it's a good idea to test your Electronic Workbench and its components to make sure there are no problems. (It's a lot less frustrating to find problems and fix them now.) Following are a couple of test circuits that, when hooked up, will make sure everything is doing what it is supposed to do.

You will test your Electronic Workbench by connecting wires to some of the springs. Connecting springs builds a circuit that connects the components.

Some Basic Rules of Wiring:

• Connect metal to metal. Make sure the wire (not the plastic wrap) is hooked in the spring.

• Gently pull the wires to make sure they are connected.

• Try not to bend the wires more than you have to. They will eventually break.

• Use the shortest wire possible. You might need the longer one somewhere else, and besides, it looks tidier.

• Last, but certainly very important: **Never hook up the battery until you have the whole circuit completed.** Hooking it up too early can fry your components.

Test Circuit #1: Red LED

Take your wires and hook up the following pairs of springs: **11 and 33, 12 and 30, 29 and 34**. Attach the battery clip, and the red LED should light up. If it doesn't, make sure that the flat side of the LED is facing spring 29.

 ## Test Circuit #2: Green LED

Hook up the following pairs of springs: **11 to 33, 12 to 32, and 31 to 34.** Attach the battery clip, and the green LED should light up. If it doesn't, double-check that the flat side of the LED is facing spring 31.

 ## Test Circuit #3: Transistor 1

To test transistor 1 (springs 23, 24, and 25) connect the following pairs of springs: **11-33, 12-30, 17-23, 24-29,**

25-34. Attach a long wire to spring 18, hook up the battery clip, and touch the other end of the long wire to spring 33. The red LED should light up. If it doesn't, then transistor 1 was not installed properly. Make sure the leads are in the right holes.

 ## Test Circuit #4: Transistor 2

To test the other transistor, connect the following pairs of springs: **11-33, 12-30, 17-26, 27-29, 28-34.** Again, attach a

wire to spring 18, hook up the battery clip, and then touch the other end of the wire to spring 33. If the red LED lights up, all systems are go! If not, double-check that all the leads are attached to the right springs.

Troubleshooting

GENERAL TROUBLESHOOTING

Sometimes you will find that a circuit won't work, even after you double-check all the connections. If this is the case, first check your battery, especially if you've left it in your circuit over the weekend by mistake. If the battery is okay, take all the wires off and start again from scratch, paying close attention to the directions. (I know it's frustrating, but it can be easier than tracking the problem down any other way.)

If the circuit still doesn't work, you may have burned out a transistor. (They are fragile little guys, I'm afraid.) Disconnect all the wires and try the transistor-checking circuits previously outlined. If the transistor is not working, try your local Radio Shack or other electronic parts store and ask for a "general purpose NPN transistor, such as 2N2222 or 2N3904." No, they don't cost very much.

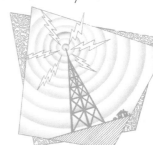

Note to Parents

NOTE TO PARENTS

These hints cover most of the problems your child might encounter. The transistors and the LEDs are the components voted "most likely to cause trouble," but the circuits on page 19 will allow easy testing of them. If they break, they are available, inexpensively, at any electronics supply store.

As you help (or watch) your child assembling their circuits, keep in mind that:

1. something is bound to go wrong eventually,

2. your child will become frustrated,

3. this is perfectly normal and happens to NASA engineers, too,

4. with a little support from you, he or she should be able to find the problem and fix it.

If a circuit just won't cooperate and you've done everything imaginable, then pack it in. Move on to another circuit, and come back to the problem circuit another day. There's a very good chance it will work perfectly. After all, as Scarlett O'Hara said (famous electrician that she was), "Tomorrow is another day!"

Engine Sounds

experiment 1

This circuit creates a realistic engine sound, just like an arcade game. Here are the hookups for this circuit:

7-35, 8-16-23-45, 15-33-36, 24-37, 25-34-44, 40-51, 41-52

Remember to connect the battery after you have made all the hookups!

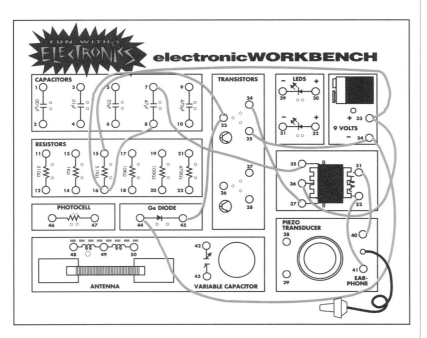

What's going on?

The noise you hear in your earphone should sound like the revving engine of a car. That's because the earphone itself actually makes the sound much the same way an engine does.

A car gets its power from a series of small rapid explosions inside the engine. Of course, all those bangs are deep inside a big metal box, so you don't hear very much—except where the exhaust comes out of the car. Each explosion pushes hot gases out the tailpipe—*pop!* When lots of these pops happen very quickly, the air in the pipe vibrates, and

makes the sound we are all so familiar with. When a car speeds up, the explosions happen even faster, which makes the air in the tailpipe vibrate faster, which makes the familiar

So what's happening with the earphone? Inside is a small coil of copper and a tiny piece of plastic with a magnet glued to it. The circuit you built sends little zaps of electricity through the copper coil and each time this happens the magnet pulls up close to the coil. After the electricity stops, the magnet pulls away, which pushes a little puff of air out of the earphone—

pop! When lots of these pops happen very quickly—hey, didn't we just talk about this?

The next time you play a hand-held video game that makes a racing-car sound, or your little brother races by with that noisy toy car that drives you *crazy*, you'll know that inside each of these is a circuit like this one.

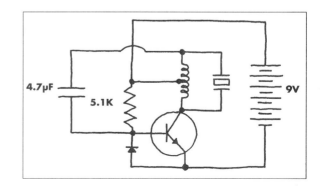

4.7μF

5.1K

9V

Siren with Light

This circuit makes a siren sound and also has a flashing LED. You will connect a yellow wire at one end and use the other end to touch another spring and create a siren sound.

Here are the connections:

5-35, 6-15-20-23, 24-37-39, 11-19-33-36-38-yellow wire, 25-28-34, 16-17, 18-21, 22-26, 12-30, 27-29

When you connect the battery, you will hear a tone. When you touch the loose end of the yellow wire to spring 18, the tone changes, and the red LED lights up. Try touching and then removing the wire from the spring several times in a row to make a realistic siren sound.

What's going on?

This circuit incorporates something called an *oscillator* (no, it's not a cross between an ocelot and an alligator). An oscillator is a circuit that switches the electricity on and off very quickly—sort of like a traffic light for the electricity, only it switches from red to green and back again thousands of times every second. The electricity turns the piezo transducer on and off very quickly, making it vibrate. That's what makes the sound. Here, you control the oscillator by touching the wires together, which sends electricity to the oscillator and to the LED (that's short for "Light-Emitting Diode"—remember?)

Sirens and flashing lights are, of course, very important for trying to get someone's attention. They're especially helpful when people get distracted.

Think about how focused you can get when playing a really intense video game. You're on a roll, you still have

three lives left, you've just reached the 13th level for the very first time, you're completely surrounded by a gazillion evil mutant creatures, and you're fighting for your life. Then you become vaguely aware of a strange sound—something that almost sounds like your mother's voice calling your name. Suddenly she's standing between you and the television screen saying, **"Earth to child! Earth to child! I've called you to dinner ten times!"**

People driving cars can get pretty distracted, and that's why emergency vehicles use lights and sirens. The lights flash so rapidly and shine so brightly that they are almost impossible to ignore. They can be picked out of a background of lights from miles away. As for the sirens, they're more than just loud. The quick changing of the sound—**EEEoooEEEooo**—gets people's

attention as well. Many emergency vehicles can also change their sirens—some ambulances have as many as 13 *different* sirens!

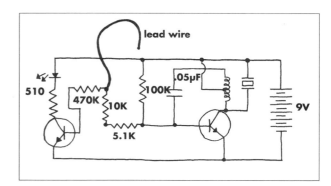

Come to think of it, a siren would probably get your attention while you're playing video games, too.

Light Fader

This circuit slowly turns off an LED. When you touch the loose end of the yellow wire to spring 19, the LED will shine brightly. When you remove the yellow wire from spring 19, the LED will slowly fade and then go off.

These are the connections:

11-17-33, 12-30, 24-27-29, 25-26, 10-20-28-34, 18-yellow wire, 9-19-23

In this project, the capacitor fills up with electricity, then passes it on to the part of the circuit where the LED is. The light slowly dims as the current flows out of the capacitor, and when the capacitor is finally empty, the light goes out.

What's going on?

This circuit uses a *capacitor*, which we talked about in the introduction. It's a kind of storage tank that fills up with electricity instead of water.

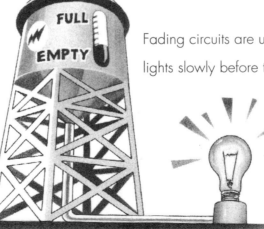

Fading circuits are used in movie theaters to fade the lights slowly before the movie starts, which gives everyone a few moments to get ready before the room gets totally dark. For instance, imagine there's some guy trying to squeeze past your legs as he struggles to balance four extra-humongous-super-large soft drinks, when the lights are suddenly turned off. You can imagine the advantages of a slow fade-out.

It's also nice to have the lights slowly fade on at the end of the movie. After you've been sitting in the dark for about two hours, it is *not* a pleasant experience to suddenly have a bunch of bright lights shining in your face.

Fading circuits are also used in video cameras (to get those spiffy fade-out and fade-in effects), stage lights, and the little lights inside cars. I always wished I had them in my bedroom in my parents' house, because I hated turning out the light and walking to my bed in the dark. I wasn't afraid of monsters—I was afraid of tripping over my own junk and breaking my neck. (My mom and dad thought I could fix the problem more easily by picking up the junk. Their solutions were never very creative.)

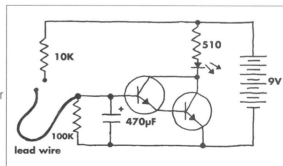

Traffic Light

When you hook up the battery, the red and green LEDs will blink back and forth, just like a traffic light. The LEDs blink faster than usual, so you don't have to wait forever for the light to change as you would at a real stoplight.

These are the connections:

**9-29-24, 11-19-21-30-32, 8-20-23, 10-22-26,
7-27-31, 25-28-34, 12-33**

What's going on?

This circuit works like an old-fashioned traffic light, which had a built-in timer that controlled when the lights changed color. These timers were mechanical devices using gears and switches to turn the lights on and off. The timer in your project is made from capacitors and resistors.

When the capacitor fills with enough electrical current, it changes which LED is lit. The size of the capacitor determines how long it will take to fill, which in turn controls how often the traffic light changes.

Timer-driven stoplights work fairly well, but it can be pretty frustrating when you find yourself sitting at a red light and there's nobody else in sight. Nowadays most traffic lights are "smart"—they have computers that tell them when to change. The computers have pressure sensors built right into the street that signal when a car is waiting, so the light turns green as soon as the other street is clear.

control how long people brush their teeth. Arguments over how long it's taking to pass the food around the table? Put the stoplight on the table and have the food rotate every time the light turns green.

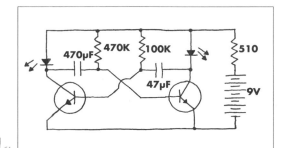

Unfortunately, our stoplight is of the "dumb" variety, but this doesn't mean it can't be useful. Big lines at the bathroom in the morning? Put it by the sink to

Burglar Alarm

Before you connect the battery, twist together the ends of the two loose wires, then connect the battery. When you pull the wires apart, the alarm will sound.

These are the connections:

3-35, 12-38-yellow wire, 11-19-33-36, 27-37-39-yellow wire, 4-20-21-26, 22-28-34

What's going on?

This is one of the most common kinds of burglar alarm. Part of the circuit is a simple switch, with one part mounted on a door and the other on the door frame. If the door is closed, the switch is connected and the current can go through. When the door is opened, the switch opens, and the electricity can't get through, making the buzzer (actually the piezo transducer) sound off in its rather annoying style.

Wait a minute! If the switch is open and the electricity can't get through, shouldn't the piezo transducer be off? How can the piezo transducer work if the electricity isn't reaching it?

Good question. I'm glad you asked. The circuit is set up so that the current can either pass through the switch or go through the piezo transducer. Either way makes a complete circuit. Electrical current is very practical, however (perhaps "lazy" would be a better term). It always takes the easiest path it can find, and as it turns out, the part of the circuit with the piezo transducer has more resistance than the part with the switch. It's no contest—the current heads over the switch and leaves the piezo transducer in the dust.

RRRRRRR!

However, when someone opens the door (and therefore the switch), the switch part of the circuit becomes a dead

end. Suddenly the piezo transducer is the only game in town. The current heads on through, and the alarm buzzer goes on.

Some commercial burglar alarms work exactly the same way—look for little wired boxes on store doors. Another version uses little strips of metal tape on the glass in store display windows. That metal tape is the "switch" part of the burglar alarm. If some unsavory character (or anyone else, for that matter) breaks the glass, it will break the metal tape, and the alarm will sound.

So there you have it. Now you can use the alarm in all sorts of ways. Hook it to your bedroom door to keep nosy brothers or sisters out (or to catch the tooth fairy in the act, assuming she uses the door). Wire the box containing your comic book collection to prevent unauthorized reading. Set up an alarm so that when your older brother tries to sneak into the house two hours past curfew *everyone* will know. (Unfortunately, while entertaining, this usually results in a squished circuit.)

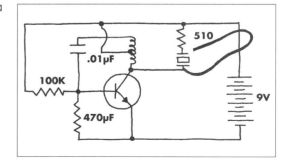

Musical Organ

This circuit uses pencil marks to play music! First, build the circuit following the connections below. Then find a piece of thin white paper and trace the funny shape below. Using a regular (not colored) pencil, color in the shape so it's really dark and there is no white showing through at all. Press one wire to the bottom of the pattern and the other to the end of one of the three lines. Make sure your finger doesn't touch the metal ends of the wire when you press the wire onto the pencil marks. Try each line for a different musical note!

Here are the connections:

Yellow wire-17, yellow wire-33-36-38, 4-18-19-23,
3-35, 24-37-39, 20-25-34

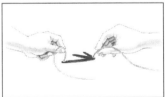

What's going on?

As you probably figured out already, there is another oscillator in this circuit. (Those little guys really get around.)

But what about the pencil marks? Well, despite the fact that we call the dark part of the pencil the "lead," there is no lead in a pencil. It's mainly a material called *graphite*, which conducts electricity. When you put the wires at either end of the pencil line, electricity goes through the pencil line, making the oscillator oscillate and the piezo transducer speak.

However, graphite isn't a very *good* conductor. When the line you've drawn is really short, lots of electricity can get through.

The longer the line is, the harder it is for the electricity to make it from one wire to the other, so less makes it to the circuit. That's why different lines make different sounds.

All of the electronic instruments that musicians use in a concert utilize some variation of this circuit idea, whether they're keyboards, guitars, or whatever weird thing they're playing this week. And who knows—maybe some day you'll be at a concert and the lead singer's keyboard will explode in a ball of sparks. He'll stand up and say, "Unless someone here can make me a new instrument, we'll have to cancel the concert." You'll grab your circuit, a sheet of paper and a pencil, race to the stage, and save the day!

All right, so that's a little much. But at least you have an idea of how the instruments work!

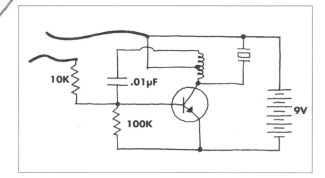

Touch-Activated Switch

This circuit turns on an LED when you simply touch a wire. To turn on the LED, simply hold the end of one yellow wire and, with your other hand, touch the end of the other one.

Here's how to hook this up:

Yellow wire-11, yellow wire-13-17-33, 18-24, 12-23, 25-26, 14-30, 27-29, 28-34

What's going on?

Don't look now, but your body is part of this circuit!

HEY! I'M A CIRCUIT!

Remember when we talked about conductors in the introduction? Well, it seems that our bodies are conductors—after all, they're mostly water. As a matter of fact, we use electricity to run ourselves all the time. Your body uses electricity to control

when the heart muscle pumps, when your lungs breathe in and out, and all the workings of all the other muscles and nerves in your body.

What's this got to do with your circuit? Touching the space between the wires turns you into part of the circuit. The current is going from one wire into your fingertip, through your skin, and into the other wire (don't worry, there isn't enough electricity in the circuit to hurt you). This works only because our bodies can conduct electricity.

A switch like this has no moving parts, which makes them pretty handy, since there is nothing to wear out or break. That's why you'll find lots of elevators with touch-activated switches, since they get pushed hundreds of times a day. These switches also work really well in places where regular switches would be too big, such as computer touch screens. These screens are covered with lots of tiny little

switches that turn on when you touch them, letting the computer know where your finger is. (Now, when the computer can tell me where I left my lunch, I'll be *really* happy.)

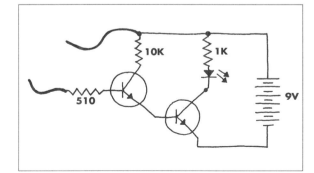

Do NOT experiment with putting other kinds of electricity into your skin! It doesn't take a lot of electricity to do a lot of damage.

Sound-Activated Switch

This circuit uses sound waves to turn on the LED. After you connect the battery, clap right above the piezo and you'll see the LED light up. It will flash for an instant when the sound waves from your clap hit the piezo transducer. Try shouting really loudly and see if you can light up the LED.

Here's how to hook it up:

11-17-21-33, 12-30, 24-29, 18-23-27, 19-22-26-38, 20-25-28-34-39

What's going on?

The circuit you have built was designed to respond to a loud, sharp sound. (Congratulations! Your circuit is more cooperative than my cat!) When you clap your hands, it

CLAP!

sends vibrations through the air. The vibrations make the disk inside the piezo transducer bend back and forth, which in turn makes a little bit of electricity. That little bit of electricity is just enough to start up the circuit and send enough electricity to the LEDs to light them up.

A device with a sound-activated switch can be used for lots of handy things. You've probably seen the ads on television for a little box you can plug your appliances into so you can turn them on and off with a clap of your hands. People who have a hard time moving around find this

SOUND-ACTIVATED SWITCH MAKERS CONVENTION.

"OK, WHO CLAPPED?"

kind of assistance very helpful. Old-fashioned television remote controls worked on a similar principle, but used sounds so high-pitched that people couldn't hear them (although the neighborhood dogs probably hated them).

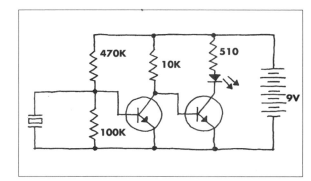

Of course, a sound-activated switch works best in a place that's normally pretty quiet. That's why they're good burglar alarms. Usually a closed store or museum is a peaceful, quiet place. Any sudden or loud sounds are a good clue that someone is messing around inside, making a sound-sensitive alarm a good idea.

For a while people bought fancy key chains that would make a beeping noise when someone clapped their hands, so if you lost your keys (I never have, but I've heard it happens to other people), all you had to do was clap your hands and the lost keys would beep for you. Only problem is, when you start clapping your hands everyone says, "Whatsa matter—lose your keys *again?*" Sometimes quieter is better.

Light-Activated Switch

This circuit uses light shining on the photocell to turn the LED on and off. Vary the amount of light on the photocell by going first into a dark room, such as a closet or bathroom. The LED should turn on. Then turn on the lights, and the LED should turn off. Experiment with different levels of light to see when the LED turns on and off by simply putting your hand over the photocell.

Here are the connections:

19-24-33, 20-23-46, 25-30, 29-34-47

What's going on?

The important part of this circuit is the photocell or *photoresistor*. It's described in the introduction, of course (you did read the introduction, didn't you?). The photoresistor controls the amount of electricity that can flow in response to light. In a bright light the photoresistor has low resistance—electricity can easily go through it. In darkness, it has high resistance, and little or no electricity can squeeze by. Your circuit is designed to respond to the amount of electricity getting through the photocell. If the level of light reaching the photocell goes down too far, the LED goes on. When the room brightens again, the LED goes off.

Of course, the most common use for this idea is in porch lights, night-lights, and streetlights. In the old days (the "dark ages," you might say) somebody actually had to turn all the streetlights on and off. Eventually the lights ran with timers, but the timers had to be readjusted for the changes in the length of day and daylight saving time. Now, however, each light has its own light-sensitive circuit so it can switch itself on and off.

If you have a night-light, there's a good chance it works the same way. See if it has a photocell and if it

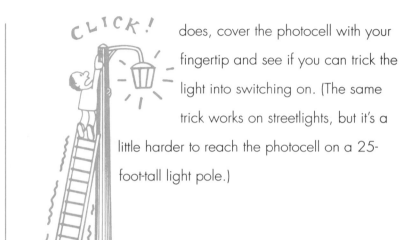

does, cover the photocell with your fingertip and see if you can trick the light into switching on. (The same trick works on streetlights, but it's a little harder to reach the photocell on a 25-foot-tall light pole.)

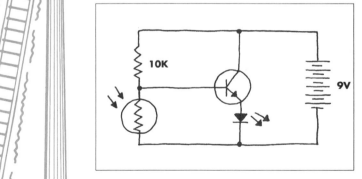

Light Organ

This is an instrument that lets you play music with light. Once it's all hooked up, use this circuit in a well-lit room. Wave your hands a few inches over the photocell to change the tone you hear. The less light there is on the photocell, the lower the tone. If you have trouble getting the tone to change, place an empty paper towel tube over the photocell (so only light from directly above will hit the photocell) and then move your hands over the tube.

Here are the connections:

3-35-38, 4-20-21-26, 27-37-39, 33-36-46, 47-19, 22-28-34

The current is controlled by the light passing through the photocell. The electricity then, of course, goes into an oscillator. If there isn't much light, there isn't much electricity, and a low tone is produced. If there is a lot of light, there is a lot of electricity, and you get a high tone.

What's going on?

You controlled sound in project #6 with pencil lines. This time, you'll use light. (**"Lights! Circuit! *Sound!*"**)

With a little practice, you can control the kinds of sounds your circuit makes. Move your hand around in different patterns. Can you make sounds like a

siren? Like a space ship? (Make sure no one is watching you through the window as you wave your hands. They'll think you're acting just a little bit strange.)

Photocells are used in lots of other ways, too. Cameras use them to keep pictures from getting too much or too little light. Some robots use photocells to find their way around by helping

them sense where light and dark areas are in a room. Photocells have

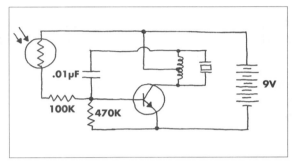

even been used in television sets to automatically adjust the brightness of the picture to match the lighting in the room. (Too bad they can't adjust for the quality of the programs.)

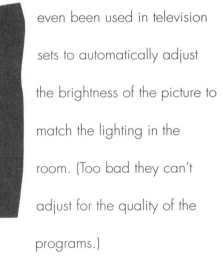

Electronic Timer

After the battery is hooked up, the timer will start when you touch the loose end of the yellow wire to spring 19. The red LED will light up and stay lit for about 20 seconds and then turn off by itself (it's normal if the LED still looks like it's slightly lit even when it's off). Sometimes the timer will start itself when you connect the battery. If the LED is on when you connect the battery, wait about 20 seconds—it should turn off.

These are the connections:

3-19, 4-16-17-24, 13-15-21-33-yellow wire, 18-26, 7-22-23, 8-27-29, 20-25-28-34, 14-30

You can also change the length of the timer by changing the capacitor. If you replace the 47uF capacitor with the 470uF capacitor you will change the timer from 20 seconds to about 2 minutes. Just take the wire in spring 8 and put it in 10, and also change 7 to 9.

What's going on?

This is another capacitor-based circuit. When you connect the wires, electricity flows into the capacitor. When the capacitor is full, it has enough power to switch on the part of the circuit that lights up.

The capacitor works like a storage tank that holds water until you need it. Suppose you were really mad at someone and you really wanted to get even with them. What you really want to do is soak them—soak them *good.* (Actually, the best grammar here would be to "soak them well," but I don't think that has the same oomph.) The problem is that your water hose only trickles. What can you do to really splash them? You can let the water trickle into a bucket. When it's full, you can

OOOOH! YES! IT'S A NEW WORLD RECORD! BY A THOUSANDTH OF A SECOND!!!

use it to hit them with one big blast of water, instead of dribbling on them.

Capacitors work the same way. Even if you have a little flow of electricity, you can use a capacitor to store it up into a higher charge. The switch that turns on the light won't work until the capacitor has stored up enough electricity to make it go.

The capacitor works like a timer. If you know how much electricity is going into the capacitor and how much charge it will hold, then you should be able to figure out how long it will take for it to fill up. By changing the resistors, you can change how long it takes the timer to go off.

By making circuits that are just a tad more complicated than this one, it's possible to build extremely accurate clocks. Many

Olympic sports depend on clocks that measure speed in hundredths and thousandths (that'th hard to thay five timeth fatht). It's not possible for a judge with a stopwatch to measure with such precision. Without electronic timers there would be *lots* more fighting over just how fast people are. (Just as my kids fight over who gets to spend the most time

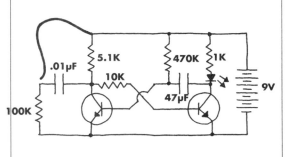

riding in the front seat. Say, I know—I could get a timer! Now, where did I get that idea?)

Electronic Candle

After you hook up the circuit, blow hard into the piezo transducer. You should see the LED turn off. To turn the LED on, disconnect the battery and then reconnect it. Then you can blow it out again!

Here's what to hook up:

11-13-33, 14-15-27, 16-23, 17-26-38, 12-30, 18-24-29, 25-28-34-39

What's going on?

What won't they think of next! An electrical light you can blow out. All the excitement of a real candle—with none of the fiery risk! And all you need is a piezo transducer!

All right, you do need more than a piezo transducer, but it is the centerpiece of the project. When you blow into the piezo transducer, your breath bends the metal disk inside,

I CAN DO WHAT YOU CAN DO.

I CAN DO WHAT YOU CAN DO

producing a small electrical current. Even though it's an itty-bitty amount of electricity, it's enough to trigger the "off" switch in your circuit, and—*zip*—off goes your LED.

So what's it good for? (I mean, if you wanted a light you could blow out, you could use a candle, right?) There are other more practical applications of this idea.

One is weather. As the speed of the wind changes, the sound it makes blowing on a microphone changes. The microphone can be hooked up to a computer that will interpret the changes in sound and figure the speed of the wind.

You could measure, of all things, how much natural gas comes into your house. A scientist recently invented a new gas meter that has no moving parts and is the size of a small paperback book. (If you have natural gas at your house, look how large your meter is!) This new meter has a small micro-phone that "listens" to how fast the gas is coming through the meter. The small computer attached to the microphone can use the speed information to figure out how much gas is being used. The information is sent over the telephone line to the company. Then, they send you a bill!

Conductance Checker

This circuit allows you to test whether or not certain objects conduct electricity. After you hook up all the wires, just touch the ends of the two yellow wires to whatever you want to test and listen for a tone. If you hear a beep, you know it's a conductor.

Here's how to build your conductance checker:

Yellow wire-20, yellow wire-4-26, 19-33-36, 27-37-39, 3-35-38, 28-34

By now you probably don't need me to tell you that this is another circuit that has an oscillator and a piezo transducer. When you touch the wires to something that conducts, the electricity goes through and makes the sound. If the electricity can't go through, it doesn't make any sound.

Like I said, you knew that already.

What's going on?

This circuit lets you test objects to see if they conduct electricity.

Do NOT check electrical outlets, light sockets, or anything that is plugged into the wall! The amount of electricity in these things is very, very dangerous.

Electricians use similar devices to check parts of things they're trying to fix, such as, say, an old television remote control. Sometimes a wire may be cut or broken, but is inside or covered up where it can't easily be reached. An electrician could take the remote control completely apart, peel all of the covering off of the wire, and look and see if it's okay. Of course, the wire would be ruined and would have to be replaced anyway.

(Oh, heck, I'd probably just throw the whole darn thing away.)

Using a circuit like yours, though, an electrician could simply touch the ends of the questionable wire to the conductance checker. If the circuit makes noise, the wire is fine. If the circuit is quiet, get out the tools.

There are a lot more things to check than old remote controls. Any time someone fixes anything electrical—toy robots, microwave ovens, cars, airliners, space shuttles, battery-powered socks—sooner or later they are going to check some part of it with a conductivity circuit.

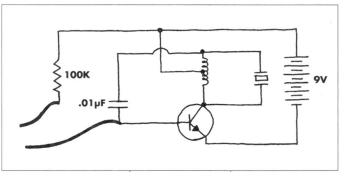

You can use the circuit to test things in your house to see if they are conductors or nonconductors. Try the obvious items first, such as spoons and popsicle sticks. Then try some fun stuff. Is a banana a conductor? How about a slice of bread? I'd suggest testing your *own* banana or piece of bread—the rest of your family might not be quite as interested in using their lunch as part of your scientific experiments!

Strength Detector

To make this circuit work, you'll need to make two balls of aluminum foil each big enough to fit into the palm of your hand. After you build the circuit, stick the loose end of each of the yellow wires into one of the aluminum-foil balls so that each ball has a wire in it. It's important that the bare metal ends of the wires touch the aluminum foil. After you connect the battery, hold one ball in each hand. You should hear a buzzing sound. The harder you squeeze them, the higher a tone you will hear. Squeeze as hard as you can to make the tone as high as you can.

Here are the connections:

3-35-38, 33-36-yellow wire, 4-20-21-23, 22-25-34, 24-37-39, 19-yellow wire

What's going on?

You are part of the circuit in this experiment, just as you were in the touch-activated switch. By holding the aluminum balls in your hands, you complete the circuit. This time, though, the electricity is going all the way from one hand, across your body, and out the other hand. (Did you glow in the dark? Just kidding.) Squeezing the aluminum-foil balls increases how much skin touches the aluminum, allowing more current to reach the oscillator and piezo transducer and making a higher tone. So the harder you squeeze, the higher the tone. That means the person that makes the highest tone is the strongest, right?

Well, almost right. Other things affect how this works, too. If you dampen your hands you will conduct more electricity. Your emotions can also change how much electricity can go

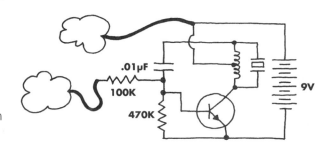

through your skin. Sweaty hands, flushed skin, freckles (okay, maybe not freckles) all change how well your skin will conduct.

That's one of the measurements used in lie detectors. As the person being tested is asked questions, the lie detector measures a number of things, such as heartbeat, breathing rate, and how well the skin conducts electricity. The idea is that if you're nervous, you'll start to sweat. All that cold, clammy, drippy sweat (yuck) conducts electricity really well. You

also get all flushed, which fills your skin with more blood than usual (which, incidentally, is why your face gets all red). This tells the lie detector which questions make you particularly nervous, such as "Who ate the fudge I made for our guests?"

Take turns trying this with some of your friends. The one who can make the tone the highest is the strongest. Or might be lying. Or is just sweaty. Anyway, they win!

"NO, REALLY, I AM A FISH!"

Electronic Rooster

This circuit turns on a buzzer (actually the piezo transducer) when light shines on it. After you connect the battery, you will hear the piezo transducer. Now cover the photocell with your hand. The piezo transducer should turn off. If it's still making noise, try taking the circuit into a dark room; if it turns off, you know the circuit is working properly.

Here are the connections:

6-20-21-23, 19-28-36-38, 5-35, 24-37-39, 18-22-25-34, 27-33-46, 17-26-47

What's going on?

The most important part of this circuit is the photocell, which we talked about before. The more light is available, the more electricity is produced.

We call this circuit the Electronic Rooster because (surprise!) you can put it in your bedroom window at night, and when the sun comes up it will beep at you. And *beep* and *beep* and *beep* until you turn it off.

A real rooster is pretty handy when you don't have a clock and you need to get up at the crack of dawn every day. However, I assume that most of the readers of this book don't have roosters now, so you won't be putting one out of work, and besides, you really don't *want* to get up at the crack of dawn. Besides, the nice things

ELECTRIC ROOSTER!! I'M CALLING A LAWYER!!!

about your Electronic Rooster are that it doesn't wake up the neighbors, and you can shut it off. (***Cock a doodle DOO! Cock a doodle DOO!*** gets really old after a while.)

That's okay. There are other fun things that you can do with your Electronic Rooster. For instance, if

there is anyone in your house who is making late-night refrigerator raids, putting the circuit in the fridge could be entertaining. You could put it in the drawer that your little brother keeps getting into. You could put it on your mom and dad's windowsill on Christmas Eve to make sure they get up on time on Christmas morning.

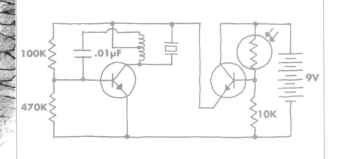

Electronic Tag

You'll need at least two people to test this circuit. After you make all the connections, hold one of the yellow wires in your hand. Then have a friend hold the other wire in one of their hands. Now touch each other, making sure you touch skin-to-skin. You should hear the buzzer the instant you touch!

Here's how to build electronic tag:

1-35-38, 33-36-yellow wire, 19-yellow wire, 2-20-21-23, 24-37-39, 22-25-34

"Tag! You're it!"
"You didn't touch me! You missed me by a mile!"
"Did not!"
"Did too!"
"Did not!"
"Did too!"
"Cheater!"

Does this argument sound familiar? I think everyone in the world has been involved in this fight.

Technology to the rescue. You have now built an Electronic Tag Detector, a device specially designed to answer this age-old problem! The catch is that each person needs to hold on to a wire connected to your Electronic Workbench, so running around will probably be a little bit difficult. But it's still cool!

This circuit is so sensitive it can tell when a little bit of electricity has passed through the bodies of

BEEEEEP!

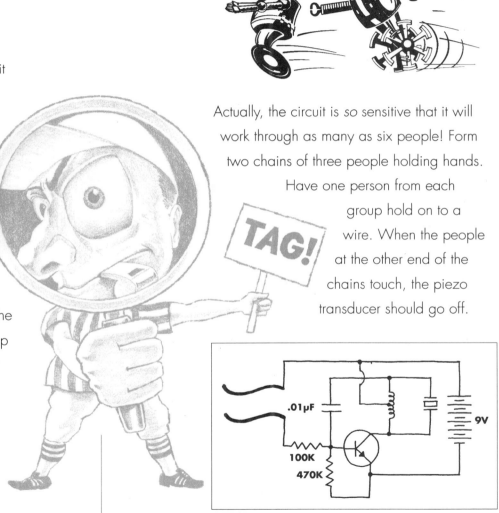

two people holding wires connected to the circuit board. Find a partner and experiment with how well it works. Does a little fingertip touch set it off? Does it work if your partner just touches your sleeve?

Here's a game you can try. Have each person hold one wire, and stand facing each other. One person holds their hand palm up, and the other person puts their hand palm down over the top of it without touching. The person whose hand is below tries to touch the top of the partner's hand before he or she can pull it away.

You've probably played this game before, but now you have an electronic judge!

Actually, the circuit is *so* sensitive that it will work through as many as six people! Form two chains of three people holding hands. Have one person from each group hold on to a wire. When the people at the other end of the chains touch, the piezo transducer should go off.

TAG!

.01µF

9V

100K

470K

Morse Code Generator

This circuit makes a tone every time you touch the yellow wire to spring 36.

Here are the connections:

3-35-38, 4-20-23, 19-36, 24-37-39, 25-34, 33-yellow wire

What's going on?

When you touch the wire to the spring, you complete the circuit and send electricity to the piezo transducer.

You now have a *telegraph*. The first telegraph in the United States was invented in 1837 by Samuel Morse, who also invented the code that was used to send information back and forth over the telegraph. Not surprisingly, this code was and is called "Morse code." (I guess "Sam code" didn't carry the same weight.) Morse code is still used today by shortwave radio operators to communicate all across the world.

When cables were strung along the railroad lines spreading west across the United States, the telegraph became a viable method of communication. Messages could be sent instantly across distances that previously would have taken days or weeks. (That may not sound like much now that we're up to our ears in radios, televisions, and portable phones, but back then this was a BIG DEAL.)

If you practice a little, you can use Morse code to send messages, too. Letters are spelled out by using "dots"

WHATS THE BUZZ?

LOVE TO TALK, BUT GOTTA DASH

(short sounds) and "dashes" (longer sounds). Here is the basic code:

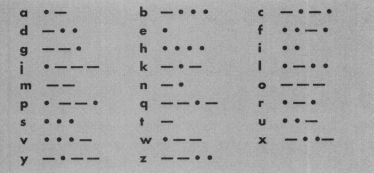

By replacing the speaker wire with longer pieces of wire from the hardware store, you can send messages from one room to

another. Here are a few practice phrases for you to send— but first *you* have to figure them out!

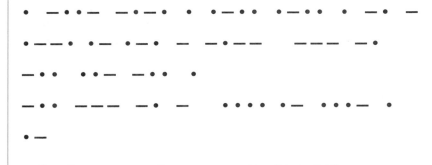

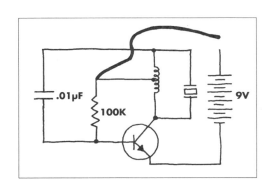

Intercom

When you speak into the piezo transducer, you will hear your voice though the earphone. The best way to test this circuit is to have a friend speak into the piezo transducer while you listen to the earphone—cover your other ear so you can't hear your friend directly. To make sure your intercom is working, gently rub the surface of the piezo transducer with your finger. You should hear amplified rubbing sounds through the earphone.

Here are the connections:

9-38, 25-34-39, 21-33-35, 24-37, 10-22-23, 40-51, 41-52

What's going on?

You've completed your own personal intercom. (You're sort of limited on how far you can stretch it, but next time you want to talk to yourself you can do it electroni-

cally.) The little disk that you talk into is actually a special kind of speaker called a *piezo* (that's pronounced "pea - AY - zo") *transducer*. Now, this is really cool. The piezo transducer is made of a crystalline material, and when this material is pushed, the stress in the crystals produces electricity. (The term "piezo," appropriately, is Greek for "pressure.")

Where is the pressure coming from? The sound of your voice makes sound waves, and the sound waves press against the surface of the piezo transducer. The electricity produced by the pressure travels down the wire to your circuit. It's a really small amount of electricity that, all by itself, won't do much, but your circuit uses a transistor to create an *amplifier* *(Hey! Wake up!* You read about this in the introduction, remember?). The tiny bit of electricity going into the transistor creates a much stronger signal coming out, strong enough to power the piezo transducer.

The great thing about piezo transducers and microphones is that they have very few parts, they're pretty simple to put together, and they don't need much

AMP

A DOUBLE CHEESE BURGER AND FRIES

electricity. This makes them ideal for small, portable things such as hand-held video games, electronic toys, cellular phone ringers, beepers, and so on. When you hear one of those cutesy greeting cards that play "Happy Birthday" or "Jingle Bells," you can be pretty sure that you're listening to a piezo transducer.

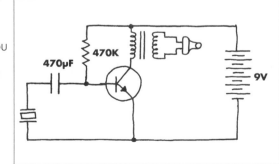

EXPERIMENT IN THE CLOSET.

If you want to try a tasty experiment, you can demonstrate the "piezo effect" with a piece of candy. Take a Wint-o-Green Life Saver into a totally dark room. After your eyes have adjusted to the dark, snap it in two. You should see a spark where it snaps—the mechanical energy is converted into electrical energy, just as in the piezo transducer. If you're really talented, you can do it in your mouth by biting it, but you'll have to look in a mirror to see it. Even if it doesn't work, you still get to munch some candy.

470μF 470K 9V

Metronome

BEEP BEEP BEEP BEEP

This circuit makes a "ticktock" sound that's perfect for keeping time to music.

Hear are the connections for a slow rhythm:

9-35-38, 19-36-33, 20-10-26-45, 28-34-44, 27-37-39

For a faster rhythm, change the following connections: Move the wire from spring 19 to spring 17, and move the wire from spring 20 to spring 15, and add a wire from spring 16 to spring 18. You should now hear a faster "ticktock" sound.

What's going on?

Ticktock, ticktock, ticktock . . .

You've probably heard an old clock making that noise. That sound comes from gears inside that are being controlled by a *pendulum*. A pendulum

swings back and forth at exactly the same speed. It just keeps on going at that same speed, swinging back and forth, back and forth, watch it swing back and forth, you are getting sleepy, very sleepy, your eyelids are . . .

Whoa! Where was I? Oh, yes. The project you have built doesn't have a pendulum, but the capacitor in it works on a similar principle. It fills up with electricity in exactly the same amount of time, every time. When the capacitor is full, the circuit lets the electricity out, and the piezo transducer beeps. Since the amount of time it takes to fill the capacitor is always the same, it beeps at a nice, even rhythm.

If you play a musical instrument, use your circuit for a *metronome*, which is what musicians use to help them

TickTock, TickTock, You WILL CLEAN YOUR ROOM.

YES... MASTER...

Changing to a larger capacitor will also slow down the beat. Switching to a smaller capacitor will produce a faster beat. If you change the resistor *and* the capacitor, you should be able to make it go *really fast*, or r-e-a-l-l-y s-l-o-w . . .

If you don't play any musical instruments, don't worry. Just adjust the metronome for a really slow, long beat. Then stick it way in the back of your brother's or sister's sock drawer and see if they can find it before it drives them crazy.

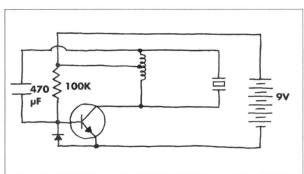

practice their music at the right speed (called *tempo* in the music world). You can adjust the beat of the beep by changing the resistor or the capacitor. The resistor controls how fast the electricity is going into the capacitor. If the electricity comes in slowly, the capacitor will take longer to fill up and will make a slow, steady beep. If the electricity comes in quickly, the capacitor will fill up faster and will make a rapid beep that would be better for jazzier music.

Crystal Radio

This circuit is a radio that works without any batteries, but the sound volume is very low, so it's very hard to hear. You should hear a radio station from the piezo transducer. To make the sounds easier to hear, try placing a cardboard tube such as a toilet paper roll over the piezo transducer. You'll also need to connect the antenna, which you should unravel completely and string all the way across a room so it's as level as possible. This radio also needs a "ground," which is a direct connection to the Earth. The best ground is a metal water pipe, such as a sink faucet. Connect the yellow wire to a metal pipe (use tape if necessary) and make sure the metal end of the yellow wire is touching the pipe.

Here are the connections:

42-48, 2-22-39-43-50-ground, antenna-44-49, 1-21-38-45

you can change how much electricity it stores) and hear different radio stations through the earphone. All without electricity! (Is this magic or what?)

So, how *does* it work?

When a radio station sends out a signal, it blasts out powerful radio waves from an antenna. Those waves travel through the air like ripples traveling across a pond. Eventually the radio waves hit something metal (such as your antenna) and they turn into electrical signals, which is why you don't need batteries—the radio waves create their own electricity. Pretty cool, huh?

This only works, though, if your radio is *grounded*, so you have to attach one of the wires to a pipe or

What's going on?

Look, Ma, no batteries!

Your circuit is the simplest form of radio. You should be able to adjust the *variable capacitor* (meaning piece of plumbing. You are actually connecting the planet Earth into your circuit! Without grounding, the electricity from the radio waves has nowhere to go, as if you had connected only one wire from the battery.

The electrical signals that come down your antenna into your circuit aren't much good at first. That's because your antenna is picking up lots of different radio signals. There are hundreds of different kinds of radio signals around us all the time, and if you could see radio waves, you wouldn't be able to see much of anything else—they're absolutely everywhere. To be able to get something useful out of the antenna, the signals are filtered by a *tuner*, which allows only one signal to pass through. ("I'm sorry, but before I can let you through I'm going to need to see some identification.")

There's one more necessary step. The signal that made it by the tuner has the sound we want to listen to, but it's mixed in with the *carrier wave*. The last part of the circuit filters out the carrier wave and leaves only the electrical signals necessary to make your earphone go. (Whew! All that work so that you can hear a commercial for a monster truck demolition derby.)

.001μF   100K

Transistor Radio

This radio uses a transistor to amplify the signal so it's easy to hear from the piezo transducer. You will need to connect the antenna, which you should unravel completely and string all the way across a room so it's as level as possible. Try this radio with and without the ground—the direct connection to the Earth. See project 20 for instructions to hook up a ground connection, if you need one. Turn the tuning knob to receive different stations. Even so, depending on where you live, you may receive only one station.

Here's how to connect your transistor radio:

**13-22-33-35-38, 11-34, 42-48, 44-49-antenna,
2-12-14-20-25-43-50-ground, 1-3-19-45, 4-21-23, 24-37-39**

You can also use the earphone with this radio. To hook up the earphone, make these changes: disconnect the wire between springs 35 to spring 38, and the wire between springs 37 to spring 39. Then connect springs 40 and 51 and springs 41 and 52.

What's going on?

Maybe we should have called this project "Child of Crystal Radio." Actually, that's pretty much what it is.

The last radio you built worked fairly well, but could only use the electrical signals made by the radio waves it was catching with the antenna. That's why you had to listen through the earphone—there wasn't enough electricity to use the piezo transducer. You can make a basic radio that way, but if you want to hear a good, strong sound you need an *amplifier*.

An amplifier is a circuit that takes a weak electrical signal and makes it stronger. (You know, like those ads in the comic books that say "I was a 99- millivolt weakling"?) All an amplifier changes is the power of

CHIRP

AMP

CHIRP!

the signal; all the other information stays the same. Advertisements for stereos almost always say something such as "100 watts per channel," which describes how much the stereo *amplifies* the radio signal. (Some of those car stereos amplify the signal so well they can just about blow out the windows.)

Making the signal stronger has several important advantages. First, you can use the piezo transducer, which is larger than the earphone, since there is enough electricity to power it. (Some car stereo speakers are so big they fill the back of a small pickup truck.) Second, you can listen to the

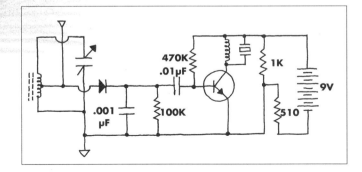

MY FINEST CREATION!

radio without having to use a grounding wire, which makes it easier to carry around. (This one, however, stills works a lot better when it's grounded, so you will probably want to do it anyway!) Last, you can hear weaker radio shows that you couldn't hear before with the earphone. So now you can listen to commercials for a monster truck demolition derby a hundred miles away.

Electronic Thermometer

This circuit electronically senses temperature. It uses a ceramic capacitor, which changes capacitance depending on its temperature. When you connect the battery, you will hear a tone. Now carefully place your fingers around the 0.05uF capacitor. Make sure you don't touch the wires coming out of the capacitor (don't worry, you won't get a shock!). As you hold the capacitor, it will get warmer, and you will hear the tone get lower. When you let go of the capacitor, it will cool down and the tone will go back to the original high tone. You can try sticking the whole circuit in the freezer. Wait a few minutes, and then take it out. The tone will be much higher because the capacitor is so cold.

Here are the connections for your thermometer:

19-33-36, 6-20-23, 5-35-38, 24-37-39, 25-34

What's going on?

"Sounds hot outside."

If you used your circuit as an outdoor thermometer, that wouldn't be such a strange thing to say. But how does it work?

This project takes advantage of the fact that heat and cold change how much electricity can be stored in a ceramic capacitor. You have used this effect to build an electric thermometer. (*Thermo* means heat, *meter* means measure, just in case you get a surprise Latin exam.)

When the capacitor is warm, it can store more electricity. Since the capacitor is being used as part of an oscillator in this circuit, any change in how much electricity it holds will affect the sound coming from the piezo transducer.

When the capacitor is colder, then, it takes less time to fill, which means a faster oscillation and a higher sound (*"E-E-E-E-E-K"*). When the capacitor

is warmer, it has more storage, creating a slower oscillation and a lower sound ("**A-H-H-H-H**").

Of course, most electric thermometers that you buy don't announce the temperature using sound. Not only would it get kind of annoying to hear that noise all the time, but it would be hard to be very exact in your measurements. ("And for today's forecast, expect highs between G-sharp and B-flat.")

Most electrical thermometers send the electric current into another circuit that changes the information into digital (computer) signals.

Digital signals can be shown as numbers on little screens (such as those on digital watches), and can be very precise. When your mom takes your temperature, instead of looking at little marks on a glass thermometer and trying to decide if it says 99.4° or 99.6°, she can see that you are at 99.47°. (All right, you don't care, but these kinds of things are pretty darned important to a parent!)

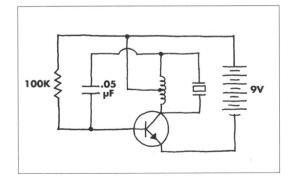

Flip-Flop Circuit

This circuit remembers which LED is lit. When you touch the wire to a certain spring, the circuit turns off one LED and turns on the other. Once the circuit is built, connect the battery, and the green LED will light up. Now touch the loose lead wire to spring 26, and the red LED will light up and the green LED will go off. Touch the lead wire to spring 23 and the green LED will light up again.

Here's how to build your flip-flop:

11-13-33, 14-32, 15-27-31, 17-26, 18-24-29, 16-23, 25-28-34-yellow wire, 12-30

A *flip-flop* is simply a circuit that is changed from on to off and off to on with the same signal. It's like having a special light switch that works with a single button. The first time you push the button, the light goes on. The next time you push the button, the light goes off. One button does all the switching, which makes it easy to "flip" the light on and "flop" it back off again.

What's going on?

So what's a flip-flop? (No, it's not what a fish does if you drop it in the bottom of the boat.) It is nothing less than the very heart and soul of computerdom. Deep in the very core of every computer, everything is based on this simple circuit.

Why is this important? Because all computer information is stored as *bits*. A bit is either a one or a zero. These little bits are recorded in little tiny flip-flop circuits where a flip-flop in the ON position means "one," and a flip-flop in the OFF position means "zero." (A flip-flop in any other position means "broken.")

Computers need a ton of flip-flops. (Actually, the circuits in the first computers weighed several tons.) Information is translated into a code—almost like Morse code—that combines groups

HEY! THATS MY NUMBER!

HEY! THATS MY NUMBER

COMPUTER LANGUAGE SCHOOL TEAM.

of information, shown as a pattern that looks something like 10011101. Each one or zero needs a flip-flop. The last paragraph would take 2,592 flip-flops!

of ones and zeros to represent letters and numbers. To store one letter of information—a "q," let's say—requires eight bits

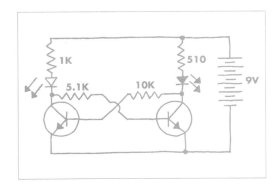

Persistence-of-Vision Tester

This circuit will make an LED blink very quickly. When it blinks fast enough, it will look like it's not blinking at all! After you connect the battery, touch the loose wire to spring 20. The LED will flash slowly. Now touch spring 18, and the LED will flash faster. Next, try spring 16. The LED will look like it's not blinking anymore, but it really is. Take your Electronic Workbench into a dark room and connect the loose wire to spring 16. Gently wave the Electronic Workbench back and forth and you will see dashes of light. This proves the light is really blinking.

Here are the connections:

7-35, 15-17-19-33-36, 8-23-45-yellow wire, 25-34-44, 30-37, 24-29

What's going on?

This project wants to fool you. You can adjust how quickly the LED flashes, but if you adjust it too far it stops flashing and just stays on, right?

Or does it?

Actually, the light is still flashing—you just can't see it. (You could check this out by building a Slow-Motion Instant-Replay Circuit, but that's in a future book called *Fun with Mind-Bendingly Difficult and Expensive Electronics*.) The reason you don't see the light flashing is because of something called *persistence of vision*, which means that your eyes continue to see a light or a picture for a brief fraction of a second after it's gone. But the light *isn't really there!* Your eyes are fooled, tricked, bamboozled.

This kind of trickery is used on

you every day. Do you watch television? You are actually watching one tiny dot of light flashing across the screen at a very high speed. When you go to the movies, you are seeing lots of still pictures being projected at 30 frames per second. We think we see "moving pictures" because our persistence of vision fills in the spaces between the individual pictures.

Still don't believe that your LED is flashing? Then try this experiment. Go into a dark room, turn on the circuit, hold it out at arm's length and swing it back and forth as fast as you can (without shaking it all to pieces). You should see a trail of little light dots. If the LED was on all the time, you'd see a solid line of light. Even though there is only one LED, you'll see several spots at a time—because your very trusting eyes have been tricked again!

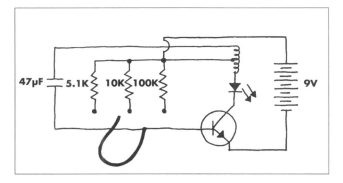

Metal Detector

BEEEEP!

This circuit can detect the presence of metal, even if the metal is inside something else. After you build the circuit and plug in the battery, place an AM radio next to your workbench. Start with the radio dial at the low end and slowly move up the radio dial. At some point you will hear a high-pitched squeal, probably near the middle of the dial. Fine-tune the radio to get a nice loud squeal. This is a signal from the circuit you just built. Now place a metal object near the end of the metal core of the antenna on your Electronic Workbench. The squeal should sound different, indicating the presence of metal near the antenna. Now try something that isn't metal, and you'll see that your metal detector really works!

Here are the connections:

19-33-49, 3-42-48, 24-43-50, 4-20-23, 25-34

What's going on?

It always seems magical to be able to find something that can't be seen—sort of like Superman with his X-ray eyes or Spiderman with his spidersense. Well, now you can do it, too!

This circuit is pretty tricky—it actually uses radio waves to find metal! The circuit is acting as a radio transmitter, and you're using an AM radio as a receiver. The receiver is tuned to pick up the frequency the transmitter is broadcasting. (Great—you've built the world's most self-centered circuit.) The size of the metal *core* (that's the piece of metal inside the antenna coil) controls the tone that your circuit is broadcasting. (Not much of a radio station, is it? At least there aren't any commercials.)

However, something funny happens when you put the circuit near a piece of metal. The metal acts like part of the core in the radio transmitter. Changing how much metal is in the core changes the tone that the radio broadcasts. The sound that comes from the radio will change too. So now you can use your *hearing* to find hidden metal!

Metal detectors have had many valuable uses. Early ones were used to try to find bullets in patients before X rays. They were (and are) used to find land mines. Many have been sold for treasure hunting (though all I ever found were old pull tabs). Maintenance crews use them to find buried pipes or wires.

Nowadays, however, you are most likely to encounter one at the airport or any other place where there is a concern about people sneaking around with weapons. The airport usually has two different kinds: the big one you walk through, and a smaller hand-held one to find just exactly where the piece of metal is.

You have your own personal detector now. How you use it is limited only by your imagination (and possibly the limitations of the circuit—it isn't exactly the most powerful metal detector in the world).

BEEEEEEP!

Find loose change under the seat cushions (hey, now you're turning a profit!). See if there's a spoon accidentally baked in the cake.

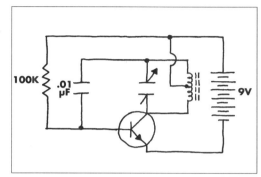

Become the Family Security Team and scan guests for weapons! (Okay, your folks probably won't go for that one. Maybe just scan your strange cousin Herndon.)

Congratulations!

Congratulations—you finally did it! (That was a lot of work, too, so you should be pretty impressed with yourself. I know *I* am.) But don't put the kit away just yet, because you're actually not done yet.

Why not? Because as much fun as it was to build the projects (at least I hope it was), it's even better to invent your own! You can take what you've learned from the experiments and try creating your own circuits. If you want, make small changes in some of the circuits so they work a little differently. If you feel really confident in how much you understand the circuits, make bigger changes or start your own from scratch!

(Please remember all the safety rules, though—don't get creative with them! Don't use any source of electricity other than the 9-volt battery. And follow all the rules about the delicate components such as the transistors—there are lots of easy ways to fry them.)

Thanks again for exploring electricity with us!

HOW TO PHOTOGRAPH CATS, DOGS, AND OTHER ANIMALS

ALSO BY WALTER CHANDOHA:

Walter Chandoha's Book of Kittens and Cats
Walter Chandoha's Book of Puppies and Dogs
Walter Chandoha's Book of Foals and Horses
All Kinds of Cats
All Kinds of Dogs
A Foal for You